CHRONICALLY POSITI

MY SON'S 5 STEP SYST

POSITIVE!

By: Marlon & Tyler Ransom

All photographs are owned by the publisher.
ISBN: 9781976747793

Cover Design Ashley McHarg

Editor and Formatter Skylar Ransom

Muse Amy Moss

Table of Contents

Dedication

To my parents, Rosie and Larry Westervelt

Introduction Plus

I believe children are a byproduct of their parents, specifically through the lessons taught, the actions observed and their constant interactions. Who my son, Tyler (16) is and how he came up with a system to stay positive is derived from his character, which myself and his mother, Cheryl have played a significant role. Now which of us has played the more significant role is a point of major contention. As a result, it is imperative to start at the beginning when I met Cheryl, and how things materialized. Crickets...the sound I heard inside my head when I was thinking about how to embark on this topic of marriage and parenting. It is relevant and it should be noted that I have always considered myself to be the best friend any woman could have, but taking it to an intimate level has always proven to be difficult, and I am talking by gigantic proportions. I spent the first part of my adult life in the fitness industry, code for personal trainer, which means my primary focus was myself. It also meant that my business and personal life were very much intertwined, which can and oft times will lead to unforeseen adverse circumstances. Note to singles, a selfish person is generally not good marriage material and heaven forbid being a parent. Now that I have set the bar as low as possible for myself, I met Cheryl at one of the gyms I worked out of. She was an attractive fixture at the gym, one of those people who worked out every day, or at least came to hang out even on her off days. I noticed her and eventually approached her, introduced myself and we became somewhat friendly.

The reason for my saying 'somewhat' is she was cautious due to the constant barrage of females in my presence, a fact I reference with humility. It had probably been two or three months since I introduced myself to her, when I asked her if she wanted to do something together, get a bite, go out. Her response was classic Cheryl, "You and me?" She acted as if it was something so out of the question, so foreign and it took me by complete surprise. Waffling and near rejection were not something I was familiar with, professionally or personally. After a few days of being pleasantly persistent, she gave in and we ended up going to a local bookstore/ coffee shop for our first get together outside of the gym.

I wouldn't call it a whirlwind romance, as I was not too familiar with romancing, but we traveled, trained, got comfortable and years later got married. Months after the wedding reception, Tyler was born, which tells you something without my saying it. His name, well, he was named after a movie character named 'Tyler Durden' portrayed by Brad Pitt in the film 'Fight Club.' Were either of us prepared to have a kid? You did read how I came up with his name right? Well, let's talk professions, I had two personal training facilities at the time with double digit trainers working as independent contractors, along with having my own clientele. She had been living with her parents and working as an RN at a hospital. NO, we were not in a position to raise a kid in any capacity, based on a number of factors stated and not stated. She worked pretty much up until her last month of pregnancy and I think I increased my workload to see her less, more so from fear of the inevitable. I still recall that night she went into labor, I was asleep when her water broke and she put in a DVD on child birth to see if her pains were close enough or whatever and then woke me up, "Its Time!" After Tyler came home with us, it didn't take long before we realized his intense and constant wailing was not normal. He was colicky, which is defined by The Free Dictionary as, "A condition of unknown cause seen in infants less than three months old, marked by periods of inconsolable crying lasting for hours at a time for at least three weeks." To say he cried a lot would be a severe understatement, I am talking screaming non-stop, with the exception of when he was in motion. I would come home as late as possible, like 10pm or later and Cheryl would meet me at the door arms outstretched with Tyler's lungs at full blast, "take him." I use to put him in the car seat and do exercises with him, lateral raises, bicep curls, lunges you name it, I developed a full routine. The issue was whenever I stopped exercising he started crying, so when I had completed a full body workout to the point of utter exhaustion, I'd put him in the car and drive up and down Lakeshore Drive. The regular time frame for this 'stop him from crying driving' was between 1am and 3am and due to the sparse traffic the police became familiar with my car and YES, I was pulled over one morning. The officer approached me with caution and purpose, as I put my window down Tyler began wailing on cue, the officer looked back at him, then at me and said, "Newborn?" I nodded in response, he nodded back, placed a hand on my shoulder and said, "It will get better, trust me," he stepped back and motioned for me to go.

Let's move on from that period, because it is making me tired big-time. When he was close to 18months old, Cheryl took him to visit her youngest sister in Texas for like a mini-vacation and prior to her return she called to tell me he had a cold. When they arrived back in the Windy City, his face and body were swollen to the point of looking like a blowfish. I am a natural born over reactor, so I freaked out and she quickly replied 'it is probably just allergies.' After a restless night, I woke up the next day and he still resembled a blowfish, so naturally we went straight to the ER, my strong suggestion. There are few things as frustrating as filling out a ton of papers and waiting in an ER for hours on end. Then there is that glimmer of hope when your name is called and you get moved to a room only to wait for another hour or two. Now in reality it may have been closer to 10 to 20 minutes, but you know what I mean. After they had taken his blood and we'd answered a bevy of questions, it was time for an answer from the doctor. It would be remiss for me not to mention I had stopped at a local Walgreens and purchased a throw away camera (Google it) prior to getting to the hospital. For what reason you ask? I took a picture of every single person who came into the room, from medical staff to janitorial services. It didn't take long for one of the 'Curious George' type nurses to ask me, "why are you taking all of our pictures?" I looked at her with several other staff and the main doctor listening in, although pretending not to, and I said, "I want a picture of everyone who has seen my son, because if anything bad happens to him...," I will let you fill in the blank. Lets' just say Cheryl was not happy and the hospital staff rushed to contact security, so I felt obligated to make it clear no harm would befall them (At least not yet). So, about that answer, the doctor told us that Tyler had nephrotic syndrome, and he followed that up with a couple minutes of medical talk, which meant I was clueless, but I knew it was not good. Now let's fast forward to Tyler at 16 years old with a couple points of notation, Tyler has a younger sister, Skylar and they split their time between Cheryl and I, come on, you knew that was coming. Oh yeah, his battle with kidney illness has been the equivalent of a roller coaster ride with an off switch that works when and if it wants to. I will be turning the reins over to Tyler from here on out where he will provide the roadmap to his system followed by his suggestion for how his peers should implement each one.

I do reserve the right to make guest appearances in sections where I have used his methodology in my life with freaking good results.

When I do make an appearance, it will be under the moniker 'DAD,' no, not your dad, but Tyler's dad. *Disclaimer: If what you read seems as if either one of us is talking about you or your current situation, take action do not be complacent!

Chapter 1:

Place an Expiration Date

TYLER

My name is Tyler Ransom, I am 16 years old, and I have been battling a kidney illness called Nephrotic Syndrome since I was 18 months old. Nephrotic Syndrome is when the kidneys filtering system shuts down and protein spills out of my pee. When that happens, it is called a relapse, and my body's response is to retain fluids that results in anywhere from a weight gain of 15-30 or more pounds. My eyes are almost swollen completely shut and my legs become like two times their normal size and I have to wear sweat pants or my dad's jeans. When I was in elementary school, 5th grade to be exact is when I came up with the idea of an expiration date. I was having a relapse and I was embarrassed to go to school and even worse picture day was that week. My dad had talked to the principal and asked that my picture be rescheduled for when I was better. After two days of being really depressed I decided I would only be depressed for one more day and then I was moving on. I told myself that how I looked was not who I was, and this illness was not who I was. I went to school on picture day and I had my picture taken with my eyes and face swollen. My real friends didn't care how I looked and for the others I used it as a teaching moment, and told them about my illness. In March of 2017, I was with a group of my friends and a couple of them had colds. A cold, is like super bad news for people with my illness, because our immune systems are weak from years of medications and treatments. I had been in remission for a little over three years, meaning I felt pretty much like a normal kid. Bam, I got a cold from my friends and within a couple of days I was having a relapse to the max level. It was hard just walking due to the fluid retained, I went from 145lbs to close to 180lbs. In a matter of days, I went from top of the world to rock bottom, nothing but sad thoughts clouded my mind. It felt like a whole new experience to me because I had blocked out the many relapses I had went through in the past.

Many things went through my head, like how was I supposed to face my friends with my eyes swollen almost completely shut and legs so swollen my once baggy jeans turned into skinny jeans. My doctors put me back on medications I had worked hard and long to get off of by slowly tapering myself off them for years. It seemed like the clear path I saw to less and less meds and even maybe the road to beating this illness had been shattered. For close to a week I was in what I call a "depression trance." I reminisced about the good old' days of taking 6 pills a day, instead of double that, and it did nothing but keep me down and depressed. It was in this time of feeling sorry for myself that I remembered my elementary days and picture day. I realized that if putting an expiration date as a pre-teen worked, it should surely work as a teen. I gave myself one more day and then I tackled my relapse with everything I had. The first thing I did was go over the things I use to do, but had stopped doing, like writing in my log book. I went back to my daily food and exercise journal, along with writing down how much sleep I was getting each night. The key for me is to stay on top of the things I can control, and educating my new friends about what I and others go through. Looking back, I know that a week is far too long, and I have shortened it to 2 to 3 days for any and all future challenges.

MY SUGGESTION

To my fellow teens place an expiration date on how much time you spend on and how much you value social media. The number count of followers you have and the likes on a post should never make you feel more or less than who you actually are. Also place an expiration date on the time spent, take a couple days each week and make real life connections and talk to friends without going on social media. I say this, because I have seen so many kids my age who get super depressed and even sick from reading a negative comment or the loss of followers. I make it a point to limit my time by having specific days and times I post and on other days I don't even go on. Follow my lead and spend more time in reality and limit time spent in make believe where so many people pretend to be who they aren't.

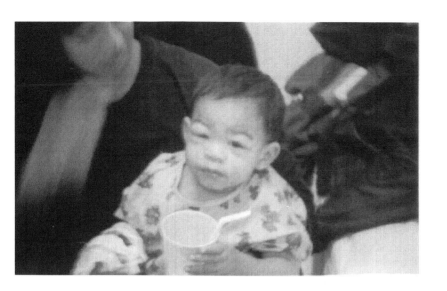

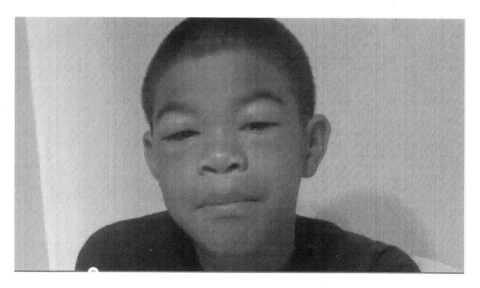

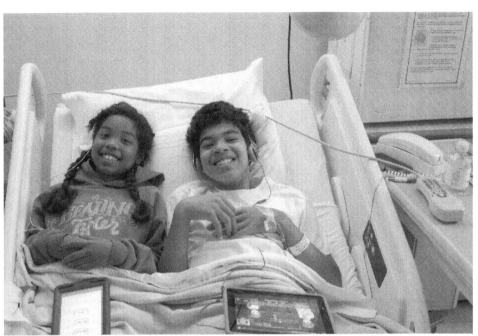

DAD

Guest appearance time! Tyler described how he came up with the expiration date principle and it is based largely on being sad, or ceasing sadness for him. I suppose it would be prudent for me to briefly describe how I have dealt with sadness as it relates to Tyler's illness, before I dive into expiration dates. I was raised in a military family with a domineering, borderline abusive father, the concept of being sad, or especially showing sadness was never an option. If you had bet that I'd be showing emotions or character other than aggression, arrogance and apathy, you would have lost massively. There are three distinct times I cried aloud, flat out sobbed and lost total control; I'll share the first time with you. Soon after Tyler (18months) was diagnosed, he spent two weeks in the Hospital. He shared a room with another child, with a thin curtain separating them. I spent every night with Tyler and it must have been around 2:00am the second night and the young boys' (4 or 5 years old) mother was sobbing, not loudly, but softly. Her son had late stage cancer and had been through a series of chemotherapy treatments and other invasive procedures and the diagnosis was not good. If you are wondering how I knew this, it's because I had overheard his doctor talking to her earlier that day and I had caught a long glimpse of her son. Writing this makes me recall his frailness, his lack of hair and his eyes, which had hope and a quiet strength. I knew her sobbing was soft, so as not to disturb us, although in reality the softness made it more powerful. I had to leave the room and I cried in the bathroom, I cried because I could feel her pain, I realized that not only her son, but many other kids were far worse off than Tyler, so I felt selfish as hell. The crux of it all was my realization of how little power any of us had to help our children. When I made my way back to the room the mood was somber and my spirit was severely fractured if not broken. In matters of transparency my earlier statement about my father being borderline abusive was inaccurate, it was abusive on every level. I do not have a smooth segway into an Expiration Date so...

To the subject at hand, when I thought of how to put this to use the list went something like this: procrastination, eating bad foods, drinking too much coffee, too many goals, not learning about investing and my ADD!!!

I know, there was too many things, so I had to narrow it down to not only the most prominent, but I also had to segment my list into two categories, 'personal' and 'professional.'

PERSONAL

Being Comfortable! I placed an expiration date on being comfortable and that was directed squarely at my personal life. My marriage was a point of major contention where as we co-existed for many, many years, void of passion we had morphed into roommates who tried to be civil with hit or miss success. The fact that it had been like that for years, I would say we were reserved to the fact that this was just how it was going to be, thus it was comfortable, we knew what to expect each day. Looking back, I saw this comfort so to speak with my parents, as they were reserved to the comfortable chaos of their marriage for double digit years before it came to a tumultuous demise. Back to mine, I had to assess the situation from all vantage points, where was I going to live, what was mine what was hers, how would the kids handle it, could we agree on sharing time with them and could we be civil amongst a litany of other issues. You get the picture, but the key was/is not putting it off. You know what I mean? Kind of like milk that expires, but you drink it anyway, stop drinking it and toss it! I gave myself 3 days and when all was said and done and I moved into an apartment about 40 minutes away, the first of many challenges was my lack of basic necessities like dishes, pots & pans and silverware. Paper plates, plastic forks and flimsy skillet from the 99cent store to the rescue baby! After about a week, Skylar looked at me and said, "Dad you seem much happier now, and I like having two places to go to." Tyler, was not too happy about the situation and it was largely due to his belief that somehow it was his fault, or more so he thought it was the stress caused by his illness. Nothing active listening, open communication and therapy couldn't clear up. Everything worked itself out and looking back it was by far the best decision made for all parties.

Cheryl moved on with relative ease and most importantly when it comes to important decisions regarding the kids we are beyond civil.

I have embraced my discomfort, because for me it was evident that being comfortable in something that was lacking in many things that constitutes a healthy relationship was not moving either of us or our children forward. As you may have guessed many things above require one to read between the lines, which should not be too difficult to do. Do not make the mistake of thinking that placing an expiration date on being comfortable can't be used with equal if not more success when it comes to your career.

PROFESSIONAL

IDEAS! I placed an expiration date on ideas in regards to my professional life. Let me explain, ideas, are what everyone has, you know when a new product comes out, a new company or investment opportunity and people say that was MY idea, they stole MY idea. You see when it comes to employment being entrepreneurial and or averse to having a boss can be a blessing and a curse. One of those curses for me has been an innate ability to stockpile ideas, like a hoarder. I whittled them down in order of what was low hanging fruit and I chose to take one and gave myself an expiration date of two days. Not surprisingly you are reading a longstanding idea that I made an attainable goal. I have written a plethora of articles on a variety of topics, and helped others with speeches, sales & marketing strategies and writing projects with the idea of one day writing my own book, but it remained in the idea stage. When my two-day expiration ended, I went all in, this book is a part of a bundle so to speak. It's the catalyst, soon to be followed by my inspirational speaking platform, merchandise and completion of a documentary focusing on my son's resilience and aspirations. Each has their own expiration date and I have to echo what Tyler stated, in regards to the importance of sticking to the date, do not put it off or extend it. An extension leads to another extension and so on, until years have passed by. It is similar to many people's health club memberships, whereas they plan on cancelling it, because they never go, but they never do. Get to work.

Chapter 2:

Gain Knowledge

TYLER

     I am not sure exactly where the saying came from 'knowledge is power,' but I know what it means that is for sure. For me it starts with where I left off in chapter 1, with my log, which includes what I eat and what exercises or physical activities I do. When I got older my log expanded to my daily medications, including the side effects, what my pee registered and what my energy level is. So how is this powerful? Well I can tell you that going to the hospital, seeing doctors and getting a lot of tests done, without ever being talked to other than to tell me decisions made me feel powerless. In those early days, I would watch how my dad reacted to the doctors, and I could tell he was scared even though he didn't show it, but seeing that in him made me scared. If you know my dad you know what I mean, he is pretty confident like all the time. When he started researching everything about nephrotic syndrome, he made sure me and my sister did too. The more we knew and the more the doctors knew we knew made us become a team, rather than just a patient. They would include me in the conversations instead of talking as if I was not there, which felt great. Eventually, when I had learned how to read my lab results, the nurses would print out copies and give them to me to take home. My reason for collecting them is so I could compare the different levels and see if there were any signs before a relapse that I could pinpoint and maybe make changes. I would say I knew I had gained a lot of knowledge when I suffered the relapse I talked about near the end of the last chapter; the severe relapse. The doctors went over my logs from years past, as they were considering whether to try a medication I had used years prior, called Rituximab. It is used mainly for cancer, but somehow doctors discovered that it helped the kidneys. It had actually been the drug that had put me in remission for a little over three years. I researched to see how many others had been given two doses of it and how bad the side effects would be.

I will say that the use by kidney patients is not extensive, so the research was limited, so I had to concentrate on what I could control and that was my diet and exercise. I knew that being as healthy as possible put my body in the best position to receive any treatment and it put me in a better position to make decisions. We decided to go ahead with the treatment, which was 4 days in the hospital with an IV for 4-5 hours each day. Boring, very boring, so I had to take my computer and school books to occupy my time. The outcome was great and I stopped peeing protein out right away and my weight went back down within days. It is great that I have been back in remission for several months, but it is just about equally great that I have a voice, and informed powerful voice. As far as outside of my illness, I have used my ability to gain knowledge through extreme research as a way to conquer school. I guess I shouldn't say conquer, it sounds like I am fighting, I would say I am able to learn things at a quicker pace than my classmates and remember the things I learn, not just memorize. All of the researching of medication and illnesses has made it like a natural thing for me to go above and beyond, so that translates to school topics, which are majority AP (Advanced Placement) classes. I use the school materials as starting points to build on rather than the only resources for the subjects. The more I know, the more knowledge I gain, the more powerful I feel about my ability to handle whatever comes my way in the future. Whether it is another relapse, getting into a great university or just dealing with life, I will always have a foundation to lean back on and move forward, because I don't memorize, I learn.

MY SUGGESTION

I would strongly suggest that instead of just googling an answer, get an actual book and read it, take notes, or as my dad would say 'Go old school.' The reason for this to me, it is makes you learn what you are researching, the more effort the more it conditions your brain. I follow that up with talking and debating about the subject with like-minded friends.

Tyler with Dr. Kamil and Dr. Puliyanda

DAD

Well, I did have to ask Tyler how he knew I was scared, I thought for sure I had always put on a strong exterior in his presence. Doing research on things you are not familiar with, be it an illness, school, or a coveted career path is all fairly similar. The ability to do research now is night and day from my youth, when I had to do as Tyler stated, 'Go old school.' Except we had to physically go to a library, look up an author's last name and find the book. Heaven forbid if the book was checked out, but I regress and I am clearly letting you know I am not a spring chicken. Due to the relative ease of attaining knowledge in the internet era, I do not have a lot to add regarding this topic, he did a great job and anything I would add would be overkill.

Chapter 3:

Embrace Family and Friends

TYLER

When I say embrace family and friends, I am not really talking about in a physical way. Even though hugs can be nice, I am talking about letting them in, letting my walls down and believe me the walls are tall, very tall. The truth is many times when I have been suffering from a relapse or medical issue, it's been those closest to me that cause me the most frustration. What I mean is they have said things like, "You must feel horrible, are you getting a transplant, are you on dialysis, maybe you should be home schooled, I bet you are in a lot of pain, you seem sad, you look totally fine are you sure the doctors are right." Those type of comments and questions make me shut down and not even want to be around them, no matter who they are. I think a lot of it is due to not really knowing enough about or anything about my illness, or maybe even they just say what comes to their mind without thinking of how it might make me feel. What I have always thought and still think is those closest to me should know more than others. I'm talking about taking the time to if not do research, just straight up ask me direct questions and start by saying something like, "I don't have a clue what it is you have, can you tell me about it?" That is a good start and it also gives me a chance to talk about nephrotic syndrome, which is a topic I know a great deal about and I actually enjoy talking about it if someone really wants to know. I am pretty blessed though, because I have always had a strong core group of friends and family members who have went out of their way to always have my back. To be clear, I am talking about family and friends who have taken the time to either do their own research or who have asked me questions specific to my illness without immediately jumping to the worst conclusions. I cannot express enough how important a strong support system is for everyone, not just those of us who have health challenges, especially when times are tough. I am talking about those who have seen me in full on relapse mode and didn't bat an eye.

I remember one time when I was 10 or 11 and my eyes were swollen badly and my legs were heavy with fluid, but I went to Jiu Jitsu anyway, at the Gracie academy. My instructor Ryron knew about my situation, so he didn't freak out, he just called me to the front and said I was going to be helping teach that day, so I wouldn't be rolling. I am not sure he knows how much that meant to me, and I have similar stories about friends at school who treated me like a normal person when I showed up looking like my dad has always said, 'a blowfish.' When you are, a pre-teen and trying to discover your place, in school, activities or even in your own family it can be scary, lonely and overwhelming. Think about how that is magnified if there is an illness involved that nobody has heard of, exactly. The people closest to me who have had my back like I said above, have helped prepare me for these high school years and beyond and I love each and every one of them. I know that may sound strange and even sappy, but it is true. Looking back at all that I have been able to accomplish, I owe it all to my family and friends who have supported me through all my hardships, and treated me like Tyler Ransom, not 'Sick' Tyler Ransom.

MY SUGGESTION

The first thing I want to do is refer you to two videos where I was interviewed by my sister. One was in 2010, titled Nephrotic Syndrome Relapse: Tyler's Answers, and in 2014 titled Nephrotic Syndrome Questions Answered (Tyler Ransom), both are on Youtube. I answer all the basic questions regarding the illness people are wondering about, but don't ask. Tell those close to you about them and see who takes the time to find them and watch them. You will know pretty quickly who has taken the time by the things they say to you afterward. My suggestion is those that take the time to gain knowledge, who treat you like a person and not a sick person and who want you to succeed are the ones deserving of letting your walls down, and embracing.

Tyler & Skylar with Grandma, Lola, mom, cousins, and aunt

Skylar & Tyler with Grandparents

Tyler with Stanley Jung

Tyler with Zachary Cruz

Tyler with Eunice Lee

Tyler with Georgia Metropolis

Tyler with Levon Alexanian

DAD

When Tyler told me this one, I wondered if he meant to say, 'Run from family and friends.' What a loaded topic, as I know far too many people, myself included who have dysfunctional backgrounds, which can result in a gravitational pull towards unhealthy relationships. It has taken me decades plus to learn to embrace those who are deserving of such action. Before I could reasonably move on to healthy friendships, I had to do something difficult. I had to take a hard and sobering look at myself and acknowledge changes that needed to be made, and make them, it is an ongoing work in progress. I will work my way to present day, but first my past friendships/relationships have been littered with my blatant disregard for monogamy and respect, along with what I call Broken Wing Birds (BWB's) and High Maintenance Humans (HMH's).

I know, I know, those require some flushing out to help you fully grasp what I am referencing. Well, there is a difference between the two, as BWB's are those that have issues, most times major issues. The issues could be emotional, physical or a combination of sorts, but they were glaring, which means it was like a bee to honey, I had to try and save them. Rather than telling actual stories I will provide a few examples: women with abandonment issues, commitment issues, drug and alcohol addiction, emotional and physical abusive childhoods and on and on and on. What I found out after years and years of attempting to save the BWB's is two things, either they did not want to be saved, or I did not have the tools and capability to save them. Take head of the pitfalls of BWB's, it will not end well, I give you my track record of failure and dejection as proof. To HMH's, they have also been plentiful in my past, but no less time consuming than the previous group discussed. A few examples of needs: overseas vacations, VIP list at all events, membership at the most expensive health club, table in the front at new restaurant openings and on and on and on. If you are thinking those examples all have financial themes, you would be correct. The good thing is they weed themselves out if and when your social and financial standing starts to slip. I suppose that is also bad, because it means you are dropping down to a lower tax bracket, but one must take the good with the bad.

They all shared one thing and that was the ability to totally drain me of many things, time being the most valuable and sadly the one thing you can't hit the rewind button on. Another shared thing is neither will ever say these things like: I am here for you, I care about you, what you want matters to me, we are in this together. Now that I have established an emotionally dangerous path, I think I will recant and share one of far too many stories where my actions caused desperate measures. Specifics will be altered for privacy of the young woman spoken about, and for safety concerns for the author (ME). Laughing not laughing emoji here. I was dating this person I will call Susan, who was a beautiful, intelligent former college athlete. It started out like most relationships, well not exactly, we moved rather quickly from dates to her moving in. From an outside observer's vantage point, we looked like a model couple, as we frequented local eateries, hotspots and traveled to destination get-a-ways. It did not take long before my actions, which were less than desirable and far from respectful led to a reckoning and an eventual break up. At the time, it was near the height of my training business, so I had a ton of clients, and I prided myself on my extensive tennis shoe collection. I had eight pair if memory serves me correctly and they ranged from Nike to Reebok and others. I made it a point to go to the apartment super late as I wanted to give her an allotted amount of time to move her stuff out. As I walked in, the first thing I noticed was the lights did not come on and not because of a circuit breaker issue, but because she had removed all of the bulbs throughout the entire apartment. After a jaunt to the local Walgreens to pick up some light bulbs, it was back to the apartment, and let there be light. To the kitchen, where the sink was overflowing with opened canned good contents, frozen foods, steaks and dish washing liquid on top to complete the mosaic. I proceeded to my closet to ensure my suits and jackets were accounted for and they were not. Where were they? I eventually noticed a window was left open, made my way over and looked down the three stories. The sparsely lit alley way and makeshift home for those less fortunate was littered with my clothing, my most expensive clothing. To which I had the pleasure of seeing many wear in various states of mixing and matching over the course of the next few months, as they asked for change and offered to wash car windows.

In my head, I was calculating what the tax write off could be, before I went back to the closet and discovered the most innovative, time consuming and meticulous action. My treasured tennis shoe collection looked as pristine as ever, until closer inspection. Every single shoe had been filled to the top with peanut butter, and upon even closer inspection with a spoon, they had all been layered with peanut butter and jelly. That was all eight pair of shoes, which was a lot of PB&J, not to mention the spreading and topping off. The reason I shared that story was to show how someone can make changes as a result of seeing the pain caused and covet positive interactions. *Susan if you are reading this, I sincerely apologize to you for my actions during that period of my life. Back to the subject matter, here we are years later and it was time to implement Tyler's plan. I interpreted his plan as him not allowing his illness to define who he is as a person, and being cognizant of those who see him for him. I had to realize that who I was, is not who I am and what I do is not who I am, and to be cognizant of those who attempt to frame me as such. I live in Los Angeles, which can be a place where superficiality reigns, new acquaintances hit you with the standard barrage of seemingly scripted questions. What do you do? Where do you live? What do you drive? When I hear those questions and my walls remain in place and I respond with the normal jostling for position and networking antenna's extended. When someone steers away from the aforementioned questions and focuses on pertinent ones that are character based, my walls begin to waver. The ability to allow people in and be vulnerable is a scary proposition, but when you lower the walls for genuine people it is rewarding on many levels. I do indeed have a core group of true friends and we see one another for who we are as people and we share mutual respect, the ability to actively listen and love without judgement. I also have a core group of entrepreneurial thinking friends, whereas our communication is strictly but not exclusively confined to business and upward mobility. If you were actively reading you may have noticed a glaring omission. What I did not touch on is family, and that is strategic, as I will be discussing my mother, Rosie and stepfather Larry in the final chapter.

Chapter 4:

Live Passionately

TYLER

     You know living passionately is probably the most difficult step for me to write about, not because it's hard, but because for me it has been in phases and has changed over time. I can say that when I was a pre-teen, I spent a lot of time when I was in remission stressing out about if and when I was going to have another relapse. I would wake up every morning worried out of my mind and immediately touch my face and my eyes specifically to see if they felt swollen, and then it was off to the bathroom to see if my pee was frothy. If it was frothy, it was like 99.9% that protein was coming out and a relapse was on the way. If there was no swelling and my pee was good, my entire being would exhale and relax. When I look back those actions of mine had spilled into other areas like school, upcoming tests would consume me in a bad way. One day I shared this with my dad and he said something to me that made sense, "Stop stressing out about things you can't control, and enjoy each day." I found out years later that came from a prayer he says all the time, Serenity Prayer, he just changed it up when he told me. But it worked for me, and it made me realize I can't stop or control something I don't have the ability to, so I stopped driving myself crazy. I can tell you that when you are constantly thinking about something bad that could happen, you never live with any type of joy or you're never able to go after what you're passionate about. It took a lot of hard work to include this mindset in the bucket with the expiration date and find something positive, something good about every single day and focus on that. After I was able to change my mindset I was able to go about the business of living and I have been super stoked to have been introduced to many different types of activates from a very early age. From karate at 3, or what was called 'kinder karate,' to Muay Thai and then to Brazilian Jiu Jitsu at 6 years old. I truly found my place doing Jiu Jitsu, and nothing I can say can explain the feeling the first time I got on the mat.

I remember getting swept to the floor, which meant another kid was able to grab or grip my Gi (uniform) and make me lose my balance and I landed on my back. I got swept countless times and I was fascinated, I wanted to learn how it was happening. You could say I was nerding out, which I still do, and that means I figure out the physics, biomechanics and muscle movement of what happened. I know my connection with Jiu Jitsu was largely about it being an art that doesn't depend on strength or weight, so much as it depends on technique and strategy. With the amount and types of medications I have taken over the years a couple of the main side effects are a loss of energy and strength levels, which are nowhere near everyone else's, so I have to be super smart about my choice in moves, my strategy. You could say it was a match made in heaven, I was hooked and I love it on a level that is deep, like heart felt deep. Now here I am with close to 10 years of training, just got promoted to blue belt and I have had the opportunity to roll with many legendary fighters and train with some of the best Jiu Jitsu instructors in the world. I will tell you that what I have learned from my years on the mats translates directly with my life off the mats. It is my foundation to which I have learned how to deal with so many challenges and issues from a problem-solving viewpoint. When you get put in a bad position in jiu jitsu, you have to think about how to get out of it, it is all about solving the problem and placing yourself in the best position to win, just like life.

Jiu Jitsu actually led me into the second thing I have true passion for and that is music, which makes me feel alive, it is like having air to breathe. I have to give my mom credit for introducing me to music, she would have the music blasting every morning on the way to school. My thought was 'this all sounds the same, there has to be something better.' That is probably why I ran head first towards the music class in middle school as fast as possible. My music teacher put a saxophone in my hands and played John Coltrane on the speakers and I was blown away. I listened to him playing and I knew exactly what it was like to freely convey your thoughts in a universal language where everyone could feel it in their bones.

It was from that small music room, as a 10 year old that my world changed, I had found something that understood me, something I felt gave me meaning and gave me the ability to express myself without limitations. Those limitations were expanded beyond my belief when my friend, who happens to be a Jiu Jitsu black belt and a musician, Eddie Bravo, introduced me to the guitar.

Actually, what he said was, "Chicks love guitar players," and combine that with my parents being tired of renting the baritone saxophone and a switch was made. Of course, I did what I think most guitar players do when they start out and that was listen to Jimi Hendrix and it was a wrap. I put in hours a day and its one of those things where you can easily lose track of time and even forget to eat. The power of music still blows my mind, and I have my own band that plays a mixture of things with Jazz as the foundation, called 'Tyler Ransom and the Handsomes. Honestly speaking, these activities have helped make me the person I am today, and they help me not only manage, but enjoy life. Any frustration, disappointment or anger, I am able to release all those feelings during a Jiu Jitsu sparring session against my training partner and friend Levon. Likewise, any feelings of sadness or even happiness, I can pull myself out of it or make it magnified with an extreme guitar solo during a performance.

MY SUGGESTION

Many ask me how to find something they feel passionate about and I can honestly give a few answers. That's to expose yourself to and try new things. Do not let fear of failing or not being good when you start stop you, do it anyway. Find an activity that when you are doing it, you think of nothing else while doing it. Lastly, back to what my dad told me, stop worrying about things you can't control, and focus on what you can control. To me those are the keys to living passionately.

Tyler with Poncho Williams

Tyler with Cobrinha Maciel, Fabbio Passos, and Kennedy Maciel

Tyler with Ryron Gracie

Dawna Gonzales-Gonzales, Tyler, Eddie Bravo, Kristi Lopez

Skylar & Tyler, Henry Akins, Antoni Hardonk and the Dynamix team

Skylar, Ronda Rousey, and Tyler

DAD

I am back, this topic I could not pass up. The concept of living passionately is interesting to me, as I have been told pretty much my entire adult life to DO what you are passionate about and money will come, or something to that affect. Bottom line is to me passion has always been directly linked to business or making money, rather than enjoying life. How many times does someone ask you if you are happy compared to how many times they ask what do you do for a living? If you are me, you rarely if ever get the happy question and one would think happiness and passion should be closely associated. My ability to truly grasp how to live passionately is in direct correlation with an unpleasant occurrence I refuse to forget, because it put life into crystal clear perspective. About three years ago I was traveling on the East Coast and the most bizarre thing happened, I couldn't pee.

I am not talking about once or twice in the morning, I am talking about for like close to 14 hours. What did I do? At first I figured I should drink more, so I drank about a gallon of water with not even a dribble coming out as I hovered over the toilet. I went to my MacBook Pro and pulled up a google search and went down the line of what to do: from sitting in a warm bath, placing my fingers in cold water and I could go on, but nothing worked. You guessed it I had to go to the one place I never go unless I am taking Tyler, the hospital. One thing I am pretty sure about is ER's are the same everywhere, a lot of hurry up and wait, with lobby areas mirroring mass zombie scenes from The Walking Dead TV series. When I finally get placed in a room, I am instructed to put on the most embarrassing garment known to mankind, the dreaded cloak that covers your front and leaves your backside, hind quarter, rear end, you can add your own word here, free in the wind. I know this may seem like I am procrastinating, which is not necessarily a lie, but as I write this the memory becomes more painful so bear with me it will make sense. Here we go, the doctor does some tests, which includes an ultrasound and says there is something blocking where the urine comes out. He then proceeds to scare the hell out of me and says that it could be a cancerous cyst and it was potentially a dire situation based on the location and size of it. Next up was the nurse coming in with a plastic package that contained a slim, long tube and bag. I was about to be introduced to the world of catheters and to add insult to injury, she was very attractive. Nothing like being in the most vulnerable position and having no say over being subjected to cruel and unusual measures. After several attempts of sliding the catheter all the way to my bladder with no success, they tried one with a curved tip. The issue was the obstruction was in the way, so the 2nd catheter made it and close to a half a gallon of urine filled up the bag. I can't truly describe the amount of discomfort this entire process caused, both physically and emotionally. To move on, I'm at the airport a day later to fly back to LA; I wanted to see my own doctor, I mean if I am going to die, I want a familiar face to tell me. The first thing I noticed was how fast people walk headed to and from their gates, with many of them barely looking up from their phones as they speed walked to whatever and wherever was so important. I noticed this, because my mobility was severely compromised by a catheter inserted and taped, with a urine bag strapped to my calf.

I have to mention my experience with the TSA agent as he patted me down prior to entry to the gate area. YES, he asked me without discretion, "I felt something on your calf. I am going to have to check it out." I close the distance with the intention to whisper in his ear and I suppose I can appear intimidating as he jumped back, noticeably frightened. That led to my failed attempt at whispering from afar, 'it's a catheter.' Next thing I know he had called a handful of agents over and I was escorted to a secure room for inspection. Yeah, that was wonderful, a ton of travelers pointing, whispering and watching me walk ever so gently surrounded by rent-a-cops, so let's move on. Now I had received strict instructions from the doctors to come back to the hospital if any of a number of things happened, top of the list being if the bag had blood in it. Well, an hour before takeoff I went to empty the bag and it was filled with blood...my thoughts exactly, I figured it's only a five-hour trip, I can make it. During the flight, back to the West Coast, I began to write what would become my manifesto of sorts based on what was heavily on my mind. You see this was what I call an ultra-defining moment, there is a stark difference between a defining and an ultra-defining moment, the former is when you make a bunch of promises and say things like, "If you get me out of this, I will never do anything like that again. If the test comes back negative I will never not wear...." The latter is one that you make no verbal promises, you make internal meaningful ones, which is what I made. I sat in my preferred aisle seat, I began writing with a strong sense of clarity, the topic being what mattered in my life, what things I needed to work on. I was amazed not so much at what was on my list, but what was not on it. It would be remiss for me to not mention the women in the middle seat who got up every fifteen to twenty minutes to use the bathroom, causing me mass discomfort and fear of the tape loosening at the insertion point of my trusty catheter. Back to the list, top of the list was to make sure my kids knew I loved them and that they were empowered with massive knowledge to help them traverse life without me. Second on my list was to enhance my active listening skills and to surround myself with true friends with mutual respect and love as our foundation. I think you get where my list was going, the key factor is all work related, topics were outside the top 10. I will also tell you that a week after my arrival the catheter was removed and I was able to pee.

I almost cried I was so damn happy and that translated in my appreciating things I use to take for granted like walking fast, like stopping to appreciate beauty on all levels, savoring a good cup of coffee and yeah...peeing. My prostate scare led me to a revision of what living passionately meant, I realized what I had always known but it made it more pronounced, it had nothing to do with business or income. To live passionately means to appreciate, take in and embrace LIFE. From the exact moment, I wake up and take a breath, being conscious and engage in meaningful relationships and conversations with people I love. I do believe that you should do what you love, but passion is at a deeper level at least for me.

Chapter 5

Give Back

TYLER

The thought of giving back is not something that came naturally, I suppose you could say I was like most kids, the S word, selfish. It is ironic that for me now, giving back or when I can help someone and not want or expect anything in return makes me feel better than just about anything else. With almost equal irony, I can tell you that having great parents was not something that led to me wanting to be less than selfish. They have always given me everything I've needed and pretty much everything I wanted, not in a spoiled way, but just well taken care. I've often wondered if my parents are so attentive and gave me so many things because of my illness, but I suppose not. Either way, I do know that having such a support system can make you take things for granted, at least I think I did. When my parents separated, I was 10yrs old and I was about to be introduced to living in two places, two sets of clothes and for the first time seeing how different my parents were. They agreed to split up the major holidays on a yearly rotation, so if one had Thanksgiving this year, the other would have Christmas and they would rotate the next year. My dad had us that 1st Christmas and my sister, Sky and I found out pretty quickly, that my dad was not big into holidays, especially Christmas. With a week before the big day, we had no decorations, no tree or presents, wrapped or otherwise. I do have to say that he has never gotten us gifts on a holiday, Christmas, or even our birthdays, so that wasn't really new. He's always told us that 'you shouldn't need a holiday to get someone something, and you should never let society make you buy things.' To be honest I never really thought about his dislike of holidays or what he said until mom wasn't there and we actually had NO presents, NO Christmas spirit. Anyway, early one morning dad gave me and Sky a task to work on; he gives us 'tasks' to this very day, so it's a normal activity for us.

I remember whenever a new movie came out, we had to take our notebooks and take notes, because we were expected to write a paper about it, or if I wanted a new video game I had to write about who the protagonist was and who the characters were and what the objective was. Back to the topic, sorry I got sidetracked; we had to research and find a women and kids shelter in South Central, LA. Why? We didn't have a clue, but we learned soon enough, as we found a place and he called and talked to them for like twenty minutes about dropping off items. We had to go through our closets, and take out clothes we rarely wore, or in some cases we had outgrown and never wore. I want to take this time to apologize on behalf of Sky and I to our grandparents, as many of the clothes were gifts from them, and we fully intended to wear them, but we had too many clothes. After ironing and folding the clean clothes and wiping down the toys and video games we had gathered, we reached out to our friends and asked them to donate similar things. We got up early the next morning, ate cereal and packed up the car to head to the shelter, which I think we all thought would be a building with a sign or something, it wasn't. It was a regular home in a residential neighborhood, and we found out the reason for that was to blend in, because many of the women had husbands or boyfriends who were abusive and trying to find them and hurt them. A woman let us bring our bags in the front hallway and we took things out to show her, and she told us about the safety issues I mentioned. We spent a little over an hour there with my dad talking to her and she asked me and Sky a few questions about school and small talk. We did not get to meet any of the women or their kids at that time, which made sense because the woman in charge didn't know us and their safety was more important than us seeing them. But she did take things out of our bags and nodded her head and smiled a lot, so I think she was like saying the kids would like what we were giving them. When we left, the car ride home we were all quiet and for me, that was my 1st real experience with giving back, and it felt like a warm blanket on a cold day. I know that sounded kind of soft, but it felt really good to realize that I had things I could give to others that they needed and it made a difference. We have continued doing things like that every other year when we are we are with our dad, and we have traditional holidays with our mom.

When I suffered a ton of relapses is when my dad created the Healing Tyler site, how he thought of it I have never really been sure, but I knew he wanted to spread awareness of the illness. We shot a lot of videos with me sparring with fighters in the UFC, and BJJ players and then I would show them all my medications and talk about my illness. As I said I know he wanted to raise awareness and also maybe get people to donate for funding for clinical trials, but it has turned in to far more than he or I could have ever imagined. Throughout the years, kids from here in the states and as far away as Russia, Vietnam and India have watched my videos and email to connect and tell me how much the videos help them. I started a video series called 'Tyler's Tips,' after I got so many similar questions from kids who have Nephrotic Syndrome or other kidney related illnesses. I talk about things like what to wear to get blood draws, *short sleeve shirts, how to do research, how to keep a log and just things associated with the illness. It is still very surreal whenever someone posts a comment, emails, or calls me and tells me how much my videos or I mean to them. I have to say that as much as I have enjoyed getting things throughout the years, it is not even close to the feeling I get giving back, and I mean no comparison. I have a group of kids that I mentor kind of by default, meaning my talking to them started out as just my talking to some kids who shared the same illness as me. Here we are years later and I find myself as the person sharing information, giving advice and in some cases even talking to parents about whether it is okay for their kids to do martial arts. I should say that I simply talk about my experiences and say what it has done for me, and allow them to make their own decisions for their kids. As time has moved on, many things came up when thinking about how important giving back is. Lives are being changed; the lonely have someone to look up too, and in general just making the world a bit brighter.

MY SUGGESTION

If you have a family member or a friend who has an illness, or any type of challenge start there. For instance, if one of your friends is getting bullied at school, start an anti-bullying group and band kids together for support, or maybe even contact a Jiu Jitsu academy near you and see about having them start a group class for you all.

I know that seemed like a shameless Jiu Jitsu plug, but it was serious. Another example is if you know someone who has an issue with reading aloud, you could start a reading group.

Things like that may seem like small things, but you can make a big difference in people's lives trust me. Start with something small and watch it grow into something you could have never imagined.

Tyler with Kurtis Kiyoshi

DAD

Be forewarned there will be some overlap with Tyler regarding the Healing Tyler site, but from my vantage point. This chapter topic is without question the most difficult for me to delve into, as rehashing past memories, especially unpleasant one's opens wounds and causes pain, and who wants that. Now, when you decide to post those past pains to paper or computer, it takes things to another level, as those intimate to the memories in question will be forced to relive them along with you. Many facets of my childhood engrained extremely selfish character traits that have played a large role in choices I've made as an adult. Looking back at my childhood, it was something I survived more so than something I enjoyed. My father was a career military man, who saw combat in the Vietnam War, and was the product of a broken family. The aforementioned is relevant as I map out my journey into not only selfishness, but disdain for the holidays. When most kids were excited for the festive seasons and all the pleasantries associated with them, I was busy bracing myself for the debaucherous, violence laden and alcohol fueled lunacy of my father and his military minions. Join me as I provide a glimpse into a childhood holiday memory; I would indeed get presents, but they were not necessarily for me. One particular Christmas, two of the presents I received were a pellet gun, same as a BB gun, but uses pellets, and a large tent, which I was excited about, since our backyard was bordering a forest of sorts. I had plans to sleep in the tent on weekends out in the woods and use the pellet gun to hunt, well you know, more like play hunting. By the way, as an adult who served a brief tour in the military where I had to sleep in tents outdoors, it is very humorous to me that I was excited back then, because I will NEVER sleep outdoors again. Back to the pleasantries of opening gifts, I unwrapped the pellet gun and within a couple of seconds my dad snatched it from my hands and scolded me vociferously, "Don't ever touch this unless I am here and I let you." Okay, there went one present that really wasn't mine, but I had grown familiar with the fact that a present with my name on it, didn't mean it was actually mine.

Same went for the tent, which ended up being what current day people call a 'Man Cave,' as he would invite fellow soldiers over on weekends and they would set it up in the back and play cards and drink...and drink. Oh, and they would take turns shooting at random things, from squirrels to you name it with the infamous pellet gun, which I don't recall ever getting to use. I use that story as an example, but believe me I have a myriad of stories from many holidays, I simply chose one that would be palatable to the general public. Let's move on to college life, which turned out to be my proving ground in emulating what I had seen in my youth. I took up bodybuilding, which included supplements, both over the counter and otherwise to go with my obsessive workouts and food consumption. This choice was a way to take back power, or rather take power, something I had never felt, by building a strong exterior. I topped out at 275lbs with 10% body fat and a brief stint as a male entertainer with the stage name 'Conan.' I am smiling as I re-read that for two reasons, I was enamored with Conan the Barbarian graphic novels at the time (still am) and I had/have no rhythm. Let's place college in the rear view as I settled in to what I mentioned in the introduction, my career in fitness. My prowess at selling personal training far exceeded my ability...no, I mean my desire to actually train people, as my true love was selling. At one time, I had two locations and a multitude of trainers, which afforded me a degree of prosperity that I am attempting to regain and surpass to this very day. If you have been paying close attention, I am sure you noticed that my activities collectively are the most self-centered and selfish with little to no debate. From bodybuilding, male entertainer and personal training or more so sales, all are things that are self-absorbed. You can also see the correlation from childhood experiences to choices made. Can you imagine what it was like for the person you just read about to have to deal with his son having an illness with no current cure? Let's sort it out, as one thing my father had me do that I carried over into my parenting was martial arts, so Tyler started karate at 3yrs old, and moved on to Jiu Jitsu at around 6yrs old. When he suffered a multitude of relapses back to back is when my feelings of powerlessness took center stage. It was almost as if I had been transported back to my childhood where self-empowerment was in short supply.

I have always stated to those who asked that the creation of the Healing Tyler website was my way of bringing about awareness and raise funds for clinical trials, to set the record straight, that is a falsehood. I came up with the idea of having Tyler roll (spar) with MMA and BJJ fighters, and discussing his illness with my filming it and placing it on the site for one reason and that was to make me feel in control, to give me a sense of power. My appreciation for giving back and eventual coveting of such practices occurred after the site went live and emails began to pour in from kids who suffered from nephrotic syndrome, their parents and others. These emails came from near and far, with some I knowingly knew were Google Translate creations. The main theme being how much they learned from the videos, be it the medications Tyler talked about, or more so what was confirmed from the interviews Skylar did with Tyler. I found myself thrust in the position of communicating with parents who were new to the illness, those who felt powerless and who were asking me not so much medical questions, but life coping ones. I cannot say that I took to this role like a duck to water, but it has grown on me, and the feeling that engulfs me when I can make someone feel better or more at peace, more empowered is joyful...it is joyful. That feeling and what the site represents had a direct effect on how I have chosen to deal with holidays. I use to simply ignore them, and then I came up with the age-old concept of helping those who are less fortunate, for example the shelter story Tyler shared, or not only feeding people on Thanksgiving, but providing workshops on filling out job applications. Out of everything I have learned as a human being, the ability and the wanting to give back is by leaps and bounds what I am most proud of. Happy endings are always nice, but It would be irresponsible for me not to mention the dark side of giving back. From my personal knowledge and from friends I will say that anyone who is attempting to make a difference, who is putting themselves and their views out in the universe and giving back, there will be haters for lack of a better word. I could give some examples of emails I have received but I am going to refrain. Listen up! Do not let negative people who do not take action, who do not give back, but simply find the time to criticize the manner and nature of your giving back deter you!

Chapter 6:

Reflect

DAD

This is my chapter, as the concept of reflection is not a part of Tyler's system, he needs more time to get seasoned. I suppose on the surface this topic is simplistic at best, but I find that to be far from true. For me reflecting had always been a source of major contention, as my thoughts were consumed with what I had failed at, from relationships to business ventures. This resulted in despair and contempt permeating throughout my soul and often times affecting me adversely. What I mean by that is somewhat similar to one of Tyler's earlier comments about when he was constantly thinking about something bad happening, only in my case it was thinking of bad things that did happen. What that did was make me think of myself as less than a lot of the time, even though I never let it show to the general public. Does that make sense? Hope so. My goal has been to take a different approach with dual purposes, one being to learn from, but not dwell on past missteps and secondly to make a real effort to acknowledge the good things done, the successes. Indulge me as I pick out three of my major points of reflection with how I use to view them and how I transitioned into viewing them in present day.

Lifeguard

THEN

I think about how I learned to swim and I hold my head up. I was seated on the edge of a pool with my legs dangling in the water, when my dad came up behind me, lifted me by my armpits and flung me into the deep end.

How many times did I go under while flailing frantically, I am not too sure, but every time I came up for air, I saw him staring menacingly at any who dared to offer help.

I eventually made it to the ledge with the most frenzied dog paddling imaginable. His scowl turned into a smirk and he gave me what was for him a compliment, which was a slight head nod. Years later as a teen I went through a summer swimming program and at the end they tested us to become lifeguards and I passed. What did I reflect on? I zeroed in on how I went to the center to see about getting a summer job, well, I went to the center many, many times, only I never asked anyone. I was too damn scared to actually be a lifeguard, and heaven forbid having to save someone. I was a coward, and I was ashamed that I told my mother they were all filled up for the summer, no openings, no help needed. These thoughts resulted in a lot of inner turmoil and pain for someone who appeared otherwise on the outside.

NOW

Speaking about my first swim instructor, yeah, I know that was funny, I choose to see him through a different lens. Rather than harbor bad feelings, I choose to consider the source and know his past, his foundation. He did not have a positive role model for a father, so his point of reference was crap, for lack of a better term. He was a career military man who saw combat in Vietnam: there is something to be said about combat veterans and the lack of resources to help them assimilate back in society. I was walking with him early one morning and a car backfired, he grabbed me as he dove to the ground, landed on top of me trembling. I view that specific incident favorably, as I saw it as him showing me he loved me, by covering me with his body. I know that is a stretch, but what kid wants to think he isn't loved? Allow me to stretch and think of him as someone who expressed love in his own way. There were many instances similar to that, which were never discussed, but I knew the reason. This is not an excuse for his behavior, it is simply a fact that I must, that I choose to consider. No, I did not forget about being flung in the deep end, well considering his history, he wanted me to be a survivor, a fighter and he accomplished his goal. Now, the lifeguard test, it was a miraculous achievement considering I was literally shaking prior to the start.

When they directed us to get in the deep end and tread water for 10 minutes with our clothes on, I thought I was a dead in the water, so to speak. I survived what seemed like an eternity of treading and then we had to take off our pants and make floatation devices out of them. After a slew of other drills, I realized I had passed, I had did it and I was shocked. I am still shocked and proud when I think about it now. Please don't ask if I can still swim, I will be forced to embellish greatly.

Education

THEN

I never really looked back at my time in college, I glanced back and each time I winced and shook my head. The period of time I spent at SWT, I had routinely called the 'wasted years.' My main priority the pivotal first two years was to get big, not to ace classes. Let me explain, I graduated from high school a paltry 150lbs at 6'1. I was always a big Arnold Schwarzenegger fan, and I worked out on my own in an attempt to gain size to no avail. When I got to college the resources were unlimited, in regards to gyms, local bodybuilders and access to enhanced supplementation with the applicable financial exchange. I met a handful of friends who shared my desire for the iron and we spent the majority of our time at the renowned San Marcos Athletic Club, lifting, lifting and lifting. When I was not lifting, eating or heading out to countless bars, I was sleeping (Sleep to grow). What I was not doing were the things stipulated in my student loans, you now, going to classes, doing course work and taking tests those sort of things. I found myself closely associated with a phrase one wears with shame, not the 'walk of shame,' I'm talking about scholastic probation. At the time when my friends were graduating I found myself nowhere near graduation as my studies had not only taken a backseat to working out, but I had become side tracked by a vocation that required late nights. It was spawned on a dare one night when there were male entertainers at one of our favorite haunts and they needed another dancer. Conan was born, with limited rhythm, but serious muscle, it was a match made in 'not heaven.'

As my friends went on to careers and away from the college town of San Marcos, I was like a leaf in the wind, living in a debauchery filled environment with no degree to speak of. Wasted years, shameful years, my mind framed them in any number of ways all negative.

NOW

I start out by focusing on what was missing from my prior vantage point and how the story actually played out. I may have been drifting like a leaf at one point, but I gained roots. If I go back further in my personal history, neither of my parents attained an advanced degree, much less went through what is known as the college experience. You could say I was a family trendsetter to a certain extent, which ultimately means I had to figure it out on my own. Back to what I choose to focus on out the gate, what was missing, and that was my decision to go back to school decades later. There are advantages to going back to school when you are no longer a youngster, like a stronger sense of motivation and determination. I would say having to pay out of pocket most defiantly contributed to the aforementioned traits. Plus, I knew I had unfinished business, as I hate those parents who constantly tell their kids to do things they have not done, that will never be me. The question I had was whether I would have to start from scratch, and thankfully and astoundingly I had grades that transferred over after a decade plus. I had to find a way to manage parenting, working and school, while positioning school as a serious priority. One way I did this was by choosing a subject, a degree focused in an area that directly affected my work and that was Legal Studies. I graduated with a BA in legal studies and went on to attend law school, which is a story for another book. Back to my time at SWT, to which I had formerly referenced as the wasted years. No, no, those years were the growth years, I grew as a person. The handful of friends I made all from different walks of life and ethnicities nowhere in resemblance to mine, I still have correspondence with today. On a side note, Dan and Clint, I am pretty sure I owe you for skipping out on our living arrangement, I will make good on that asap. I think about my ability to function on my own, and make life choices, both good and mostly less than favorable, but they were my own. I am thankful that my 'get big' goal was accomplished, as I reached a walk around weight of near 265lbs of mainly muscle and more importantly I suffered few medical setbacks.

Overall I look back and I do not see a failed attempt at college, I see a time of extreme growth, with the one constant being my continued lack of rhythm. I needed that period to have a point of reference on what not to do, on how to appreciate the ability to gain knowledge and of equal importance, how to put that knowledge to use. Those years resulted in learning on a curve, and learn I did.

Marlon Arithmetic

THEN

"Marlon Arithmetic' had haunted me for more years than I care to remember. Before you pull up a google search, Stop, I will tell you and with pristine clarity. It is a formula where I recall with pinpoint accuracy an amount I blew through foolishly and I put it up against and subtract from current bills and debts. Okay, I have a couple instances that I can share which are family friendly, first one being tickets. I am speaking of professional wrestling tickets and we are talking in large abundance. I was a huge pro wrestling fan from youth to well I will always be a fan of sorts, for reasons to be discussed. Whenever a big promotion came to Chicago, I had a hook up, meaning a ticket person who made sure I got the best available seats. We are talking about a purchase on average of 10+ tickets per month at $300.00 per, and yes, they were front row. We were easy to spot, everyone had on a Bodies for Ransom t-shirt and you better believe I basked in the glow of being big man on campus. Do the math, and keep in mind that was for well over a year, maybe closer to two years. I have to add how pissed I was when Michael Jordan retired from the Bulls, because that caused my per ticket fees to double, so it was $600.00 and my hook up had to cut down on how many he sold me, because he was selling front row to others for a grand a piece. What does that have to do with MJ? Well the high rollers who use to go to all the Bulls home games, switched to wrestling and would purchase front row seats at premium prices and half the time they didn't even show up till midway through and left before the main event. It was like gentrification for real wrestling fans as they drove fees up and it sucked. Back to adding up my cost, which I did with frequency and the amount would easily eliminate things like college loan debt, or could have been used to invest in property.

You can see how quickly I would go down the financial rabbit hole. I'm going to join another one here, as it follows a similar vein; personal training. During my years working in the fitness industry, I use to do seminars teaching trainers how to sell. I would start out by showing a copy of my company's tax returns on the screen, and it was from our most successful year, when my entity had grossed near $600,000. My line was, "Has anyone in here made that much in a year? If so please hold up your hand, come on raise it up high. Nobody?

Well, we have established you do not know as much as you thought before you came here today, so let's begin." I know the opening was pompous, but it was also effective, as it got their interest and most importantly relieved them of their egos. When I reflect on the amount generated, I formerly only thought of the gross and dreaded net differential, which made me feel like a complete and utter failure. On paper Bodies for Ransom had indeed grossed over half a million, now when you pay the trainers, general expenses and taxes, not to include living lavishly and profits are depleted. At one time, I had two apartments in a high rise, one on the 55th floor that had a panoramic view of the lake and Wrigley Field (FYI, I hate the Cubs), and another apartment on the 54th floor. Who does that when one could have purchased a condo or home? Exactly! I also had my own personal shopper who would purchase my clothes monthly for a fee, a fee that I am choosing to not recall. I spent money as quickly as it came in and many times I spent it before it came in. I specialized in items that depreciated in value, like old school corvettes, where mechanics say, "I have to order that part," whenever it broke down, which was on the regular. Now add up those things, not to mention tax penalties and stack those fees up against bills.

NOW

I don't focus on the amount I spent on wrestling tickets, I think about the comradery it cultivated amongst us. It would be remiss if I did not provide a back story regarding my love for wrestling. In reference to my youth I do not have a lot of happy memories, but I did have the innate ability to paint a loving picture around the one activity my dad did with me and that was go to pro wrestling events.

I always chose to suppress the memories of the many times we had to leave, or be escorted out prior to the main event, because of outlandish behavior. Enough said. Without question, those childhood memories motivated me to not only go to matches, but to take friends and sit in the front row. You could say it allowed me to change the past and make it enjoyable, make new memories associated with wrestling where I made sure to stay and not only watch the main event, but watch them take the ring down. When I view it like that the amount I spent was like therapy and thus well worth it, as it was an investment into my mental health.

Now to the business of personal training, where I was not the best owner, and surely nowhere near a good manager. But I was without debate a master salesman and I prided myself on that, as well as my ability to teach others how to sell. I look back on the money spent wantonly as a valuable life lesson not to be repeated; it doesn't matter if you make a million, if you spend over a million. I do not discount that valuable lesson, I simply shift my focus to the fact that my entity, Bodies for Ransom generated over a half a million dollars in one year. What an achievement, for all involved, as it was a collective effort. I also think about how to best utilize resources with any future venture and the value of being a responsible business man. When I think about it the many mistakes I made were the best proving ground and the best cautionary tale for myself, my kids and others.

Chapter 7:

Thanks, Before Death (TBD)

DAD

TBD means exactly what it stands for; to thank people before they are dead. I think it must be an unwritten rule or some morbid custom to wait until someone is dead before praising them, and espousing their virtues. I have been guilty of this myself, as a few friends and mentors have passed away unexpectedly, hell some of them were expected truth be told. I never got around to telling them how much they meant to me, or what they had done for me, be it from a personal or professional capacity. It was not for a lack of wanting to thank them, it was simply putting it off until the time was right or the next time I saw them. I want to take the time now to personally thank those who have helped, provided insight, allowed me to grow and or who showed me love when I may or may not have deserved it. With age, and more so the wisdom I have attained, I have learned a valuable lesson that I will share with you. If you don't like someone, let's take it to the extreme and say you hate them, but at one time they were your friend, a romantic partner, or even a family member. Do not discount what they may have contributed to your life, because the feelings you have now, are not what they have always been. That does not mean to discount whatever actions caused the ill will, it means to acknowledge that there were positive things attained prior to the current state of affairs.

When I was coming up with people I wanted to thank I realized something...I am blessed, truly blessed. There are a multitude of people who deserve thanks and many of them I am going to personally reach out to and do just that, and yes, I am placing an expiration date on when to do it. So how did I decide who to write about, who to thank? Well, I decided to choose a handful of people who have not only played major roles in my life, but who I have also known for over at least a decade or more.

The reason for the length of time caveat is it helps narrow down my list; so here goes it a few people to thank in no particular order, except the person in 1st position. I will follow that up with an article/interview of Tyler conducted by BJJ LEGENDS Magazine, where he discusses three important people in his life. That interview will be followed by a thank you list, with names; however, that list is no less significant than those you are about to read.

THANK YOU:

Cheryl Rabara Ransom:

YOU are without question a jewel a treasure; I was never in a position emotionally or otherwise to truly appreciate. My failure as a husband is something I will always look back on with a heavy heart. I take from our time together a slew of positives, starting with a better understanding of being financially prudent, I am nowhere near at your level, but I do exercise some restraint. Traveling does not require a multitude of luggage, one carry on and one medium sized roller is sufficient. It is best to keep all pertinent documents, such as medical records, school records, passports in a designated area. Being late is not a mortal sin that should be punishable in a court of law. One doesn't have to always talk to get their point across, and the lack of being a loquacious speaker, doesn't mean one loves less. There are other things, but those are the most prominent and I would be less than truthful if I said I didn't wish for a do over more times than not. Thank you, and I wish you nothing but the best.

Rosie and Larry Westervelt:

It is not by accident that I am grouping you two together, as you are the quintessential couple. It would be right to start with you mother, but I will start with Larry. I have to address the title, stepfather, a title that I think demeans those who may not be the biological parent, but they are the parent, the father in every way imaginable. Larry, the integrity, character and love that you exhibit is something I have always marveled at, I've coveted it. You have shown me what being a man is, how to walk with God, and how to be a steady force when winds are blowing out of control. If I had a quarter for all the times I have said to myself, "I wish Larry had raised me," I could do a lot of laundry. Thank you. Mother, there is not enough space on this document for me to fully express the love and appreciation I have for you. It took me until well into my adulthood to grasp and discern the many sacrifices you have made on my behalf.

I recall the far too many times I heard you crying, be it in Germany, South Carolina, or Texas. Your unhappiness in a brutal marriage was your cross to bear, in hopes that your son would have a better life. Mother, it was not in vain, I attained massive knowledge from traveling in my youth, living in other countries and states, experiencing different cultures and learning languages aside from English. You made sure I was equipped to deal with the world in all its beauty and harshness. I am blessed to have you as a mother and I am beyond blessed that I am able to embrace you at my advanced age and let you know the Queen that you are, I love you and Thank you!

Dr. Elaine S. Kamil, Dr. Dechu P. Puliyanda,

you have both worked in tandem for years in the care of Tyler in this seemingly endless battle. If you think for a second I don't know how difficult it has been at times dealing with me, you are mistaken. Thank You! Thank you not only for your insight and expertise, but for your forthrightness, as I for one need brutal honestly. I also want to thank you for being genuinely good people, not just superior doctors, but good people. Of course, I would prefer my son had never been stricken with this illness, but having you both as his doctors has been a blessing in every sense of the word. You both will forever be a part of the Ransom family and I speak for all of us when I say we love you.

Morgen Skye:

Morgen, the ability to love someone and do what is best for them is a difficult task especially when pride and ego are involved. You should be proud, as we are all proud of the woman you have blossomed into and the mother you have become. Please know that rarely a day goes by when I do not second guess my decision, which I know ultimately was the best for all, most importantly for you. I want to thank you for providing so much love to those around you and never think for a second that you are not loved by me.

Celestine Wills:

Celestine, you and I have shared a secret for many, many years and it epitomizes the person you are. You are the Rock of Gibraltar in a community that desperately needs you to this very day. You are not only my cousin and barber, you were my savior. As I sat with you discussing my first year at Southwest Texas State you listened intently and with honest concern. My dilemma was an age old one, how could I go back for my second year, as my GPA had taken a nose dive, which in turn triggered financial aid to be pulled. You did not hesitate in providing me the finances to go back to school, and I have never forgotten your magnanimous gesture. If you had not helped me it is a safe bet that I may not be where I am today. My family and I owe you a massive debt of gratitude for your selfless act, and I will see you sooner rather than later. I love you and Thank You!

Proshad Ramtin:

Family, the epitome of a family is people that accept one another for who they are, support one another and love unconditionally. For decades, you have been my sister, the person I am there for, the person who is there for me and the person with whom I can be vulnerable and transparent. It is rare when the amount of time and the quality of time are in sync, with both being of equal significance, our time together mirrors that assertion. Thank you for being family to me, thank you for your unwavering love, which I know has been difficult at times. I love you.

Brian 'Goose' Davis:

It is imperative that you know the many years I have known you and sat in your chair I have received far more than superior haircuts. It has been and is a refuge from life's stresses, a place where I can do something I rarely do...relax, and that is sincerely appreciated. Goose, the journey from client, friend to business associate has been a joyful and learning experience. The conversations we have shared, the life lessons we have learned and the friendship we have cultivated are to be celebrated.

Your drive to better yourself and achieve great things is an inspiration to me, and I strive to be on a similar path. Thank you for your friendship it is not something I take for granted.

Michele Fambro:

Michelle, (long pause), you have been and are one of if not the most important person in my life. You have been privy to my highs and lows, provided a sympathetic ear and shared in my excitement. Where as many provide lip service as support, your actions have spoken volumes and have never been unappreciated. Your steadfast and unwavering belief in my ability to regain status and prosperity has many times kept me in the fight. Michelle, thank you for going above and beyond in your efforts to keep me on course and your passionate belief in my abilities and in me as a person. A better person I do not know. Much love and Thank you!

Steven Harris:

Steven, I wonder if you are wondering why you are on this list. Well, you played a major part, in many of the accomplishments I attained during my years in the fitness industry. When you chose to make me a trainer at 25 East Washington, it was a gamble on your part, this I know. I took note of your natural charisma and I watched how you carried yourself, how professional you were. I emulated aspects of what I saw from you and the rest is our history with Bally's, which I know we both have similar good and less than favorable memories. Despite all that occurred in our past the one constant is the respect I have always had and still have for you. I would seriously hope that we remain friends with our time remaining on this earth. Thank you for all that you did for me, it means so very much to me and my family.

Jackie Weinberg:

Jackie-Baby! Damn I love you girl. There are times in life when you click with someone that maybe you shouldn't when you consider all the factors, to which we have a few. So much appreciation for your always being there to help in regards to helping with my vast business ventures throughout the years, and more importantly your passionate work for Tyler (Healing Tyler). I owe you far more than I can afford for your magnanimous actions and your warm heart. Thank you Jackie-Baby, thank you for everything and you know I love you.

Linda Leonard:

Many people may use the term 'Angel' when referencing a good friend, but for me the meaning carries significant weight. Linda, you have been an Angel in every sense of the word, as if dare I say, God himself placed you in my life. I wonder if you are aware of the many times I have reached out with self-doubt and worry only to hear your words of encouragement and immediately feel uplifted. Linda, you have a gift, a gift that results in not only myself, but those around you feeling like life is worth living. I am so not joking, as I am aware the aforementioned statement may sound verbose. A day does not go by without my shaking my head and smiling when I think about you and the beautiful daughters you have raised into amazing women. Love you and Thank you for being you, thank you for being my friend, my trusted friend.

Robert Mclearren:

Hey Bro! I am pretty sure we have used that greeting for well over a decade. Robert, throughout the years it is difficult for me to recall many days where we have not spoken on countless occasions. What started out as a straight up business relationship has morphed into a friendship, a true friendship. I appreciate you Robert, and not just because you are the only person I have been able to work with without incident for an extended period of time. Your ability to be an active listener combined with your straight forward commentary has been refreshing and coveted in a world where few people say what they mean.

I want to say with everything I have; Thank you my friend for all that you have done for me and for Tyler, you are more than a friend, you are a brother.

Susie Hsu Chao:

ShaShong, this is DaShong! Oh, how often I have left that message for you, throughout the years. What a special place in my heart you hold, as you have been something few have in life, a real friend. I am aware my life has often walked hand in hand with loads and loads of drama, and you have been steadfast in support, and letting me know when I am in the wrong, but supportive none the less. I will always be here for you and will always think of you and say, Thank You, and I love you.

Betsy Davis:

A better friend and confidant I do not know. Going through life with you as my friend, is the best present I could have. To love without judgement, offer advice, an ear to listen intently and to know that person is there if needed. I am describing you and the friendship we have, which I do not take for granted. Much love for you, Thank You Betsy.

Page Joseph Falkinburg:

Yo D! It would take me a very long time to write all the history we share. I must admit I saved you for last, because of reasons we are both aware. For close to two decades we accepted one another's character traits, be them good, bad and extreme. Know this, time is fleeting and there is no way I would allow any current emotional state stop me from letting you know how much I appreciate the friendship we had. I will always have love in my heart for you, and there are a multitude of memories I will deeply cherish. Thank You.

Tyler has had the opportunity to train with some of the best Jiu Jitsu professors in the world, three being Ryron Gracie, Eddie Bravo and Rubens 'Cobrinha' Maciel. I owe each of them and many of those who took time out of their schedules to roll with Tyler a massive debt of gratitude. I wanted to share Tyler's thoughts from years past regarding the three professors I mentioned, as it shows the profound effect they have had on his life on and off the mats.

Interview Tyler with BJJ LEGENDS MAGAZINE

"When I do Jiu-Jitsu it's like I'm on another planet, I don't worry or think about anything else," says Tyler Ransom. This 12 year-old Jiu Jitsu player has been battling a kidney illness called nephrotic syndrome since he was two years old.

When it comes to actual training he has trained with a virtual who's who of the sport, from Ryron Gracie of the Gracie Academy, Eddie Bravo of 10th Planet Jiu Jitsu and Rubens Cobrinha Charles of Cobrinha BJJ. He credits each of them with not only teaching him on the mat, but also off it, specifically in his battle against chronic illness.

BJJ: Tyler lets start with Ryron Gracie, what have you learned from him.

Tyler: Well, when I started training at the Gracie Academy there were a lot more kids than I was use to and some of them were better than me. I had come from an academy where I was better than the other kids and I rarely if ever had to tapout. The first couple of weeks at the Gracie's I refused to tap when I would get caught and I would cry not because I was hurt, but because I was angry and upset. One day Ryron talked to me when were about to leave and he had seen me crying, he saw everything that happened when I was sparring.

He told me that when he was a kid he got tapped out all the time and that it helped him learn, it helped him learn how not to get caught in the move that was used. Basically what I took from that was getting tapped out was actually a good thing, because I learn from it and I learn defenses to it for the next time I roll.

I use the same principle when I suffer a relapse, I don't get too sad, I kind of see it as getting tapped and I just try and learn from it by writing down what I ate like a week leading up to getting sick, were any of my friends sick, did I take all of my meds. I just think about defenses and how to get better, and have better defenses.

BJJ: What about Eddie Bravo, start with how you met him if you can recall?

Tyler: I met Eddie when I was almost nine years old at the Legends MMA gym. I talked to him and his class about my illness and I was so scared I am not even sure what I said. I felt a lot more comfortable when I rolled with him and then I rolled with UFC fighter George Sotiropoulos who Eddie was training. What I learned from Eddie is it is okay to be different and being different is not a bad thing. To be honest I use to feel bad, because I was different than my classmates, with having to take medications and constant doctor appointments and a special diet. I saw that Eddie had created his own style of Jiu Jitsu with cool names for the moves and he doesn't wear a gi. Now I think that being different actually makes me stronger than a lot of kids who don't have to deal with things that I have to. Eddie is also a musician, and I am too, I play the saxophone, so we are similar in a lot of ways I think and he is my friend.

BJJ: That leaves us with your present instructor Cobrinha, what have you learned from him?

Tyler: When I met Cobrinha I saw all of his medals and trophies at his academy and I was super impressed. The truth is when I started training there I had grown really tired of taking my meds every morning and every night and all the other things I have to do. It had become like a chore to stay on track. I have learned from watching what Cobrinha does every day I am there to train or watch my sister train. He is not only very positive all the time, but he works so hard in drilling and in teaching classes. When I see him I always think that I should be more disciplined and work harder, because I see how someone like him has won as much as he has.

I know that many people want to win, but if they saw how hard he works I don't know if they would do it, so I learn from him that if you work hard you see results.

BJJ: Do you have anything to say to all of the people who follow you on your website or Facebook page?

Tyler: Thank you for liking my page and for checking out my website and for donating or just posting nice things. I also want to say that all proceeds go to the Nephcure Foundation a non-profit organization searching for a cure and it helps kids all over the world who are battling this a long with me.

It should be noted that many of you have supported our effort to bring Tyler's story, his tenacious battle against kidney illness to fruition and the documentary will be completed and released before the end of 2018. That is of course barring any unforeseen adverse circumstances.

THANK YOU!

Ebie Rabara, Emiliana Ayat, Deb Blyth, Erin Herle, Karen Tran, Karna Nelson, Jane Minondo, Edward Pulidindi, Dmitriy Smolensky, Robyn Jolicoeur, Steven Bright, Troi Valencia, Tiana Heggins, Yuko Ishikawa, Marc Leavitt, Franck LOUIS-MARIE, Frank Davis, Luis Alvarez, Derek Kaivani, Bean Makar, Seong Yang, Monica Martinez, Rob Adler, Kris Shaw, Michael Leonard, Michelle Reddell, Dave Orth, Richard M Pujol, Leonard Song, Joe Gillis, Chong Bennett, Jacob Shneiderman, Sharlane Bailey, Henriette Werner, Jason Otero, Jessica Young, Cora Sek, Don Schmelhaus, Joshua McAdoo, Genevieve Vogelgesang, Mark Kelland, Kimberly Page, Jennifer Jolicoeur, Elizabeth Collins, Cat Arnett, Cliff Able, Garett Sakahara, Joan Trimble, Blanca Marisa Garcia, Mary Callicoat, Christina Russell, David Abernathy, Matt Hancock, Craig Funk, Dean O'Donnel, Daniel Yeardye, Fabiano Iha, Amy Moss, Craig Clement, Deanna Chan, Myles Leevy, Amos Pizzey, Elbert Thomas, Evan Townsely, Ronald Devilla, Fabbio Passos, Kennedy Maciel, Daniela Maciel, Mark Nagel, Greg Silva, Maggie Lin, Alexia Harris, Ronda Rousey, Henry Akins, Fabricio Werdum, Renato Babalu Sobral, Dan Hardy, Enson Inoue, George Sotiropoulos , Isaac Doederlein, Levon Alexanian, Guy Thompson, John Horvath, Ram Ananda, Vidal Trujillo, Shalome McCarty, Alan Jouban, Alvaro Roble, Dawna Gonzales-Gonzales, Jordan Collins, Jarrod Kwity, Antoni Hardonk, Rener Gracie, Rorion Gracie, Racquel Kussman, Kenny Jewel, Niki McElroy, Nancy McLellan, Luke Hawx, Glen Isobe, Kimberly Leaonard Page, Brittany Leaonard Page, Rehan , Shawn Hammonds, Leila Manzano Ayat, Efren Ayat, Alex Stuart, Mollii Khang, Steven Romero, Savant Young, Joshua McAdoo, Ralek Gracie, Pastor Vincent Dehm, Johnny Tama, Geofrey Van Haeren, Louie Rabara, Rom Rabara, Nyjah Rollins, Dian Moy, Aaron Woolfolk, Seymour Yang, Vince 'Bear' Quitugua, Stefan Struve, Mark Munoz, Denise Granito, Jesus Bryant, Loredana Nesci, Brittany Leaonard Page, Kyle 'The White Wolf' Cox, Maricel Sarmiento, Samuel Smith, Kristina Barlaan, Stephanie Singson, Jim Hevner, Michael Carnes, Lefco Stefanos, Marcus Geeter, Jennifer Shneiderman, Bob Crowley, Kenny Jewel, Lelia Manzano Ayat, Spencer Lazara, Bryan Burk, Cliff Able, Monica Martinez, Enson Inoue, Joshua McAdoo, Henriette Werner, Jhonny Tama, Pastor Vincent Dehm, Ken Furth, Sadie Rose, Tove Soderstein, Stoney Lee Grimes, Bret Stevens,

Bruno O'Hara, Jacqueline Batalis, Sally Delgado, Keith Ledford, Lavera Mayfield, Evangeline Rabara Treadwell, J.J. Ancheta, September Redecki, Garrett Weaver, Yuri Rutman, Bruce Hathcock, Milan Bakic, Kali Wata, Cheick Kongo, Nate Noggle, Julie Kahlfeldt, Sheryl Zimmerman, Jeff Nason, Andrew t. Glass, Anita Bryant Mauro, Ronda Rowe, Don Schmelhaus, Jhonny Loureiro, David Coury, Wayne Ashford, Gary Cooper, Jeff Borkoski, Glenn Shishido, Nan Rochelle Erlich Smith, Marc Smith, Amy and Robert Hernandez, Mayra Mazza, Raven Miles, Jerry Wilson, Caio Malta, Judy Kasner, Lars Nelson, Kevin Quinn, Carole Schore, Pieter Buist, Juanito Ibarra, Wilner & O'Reilly...Stanley Jung, Eunice Lee, Georgia Metropolis, Andrew Coda, Bram Silbert, Jacob Shneiderman, Alek Hughes, Michael Chino, John Lopez, Ian McCambridge, Freya Marr-Johnson, Jack Houlihan, Melina Garcia, Eddy Sarabia, Zachary Cruz, Shane P. W., Adam Schiller, Percy Gonzalez, Jarred Asars,, Illan Tubis, Jared Martin, Kotama Estall, Adam Thomas, Eden Mohabber, Chae Kim, Ally Hong, Caylen Monreal, Patrick Yoon, Sarah Mandt, Juan Brambila, Chris Lee, Sal Oxford, Hannah Levine, Sophia Roybal

.and to anyone I have missed, trust me it was not intentional, Thank You.

GET IN TOUCH

"Stop Waiting and Start Doing!"

Finger pointing picture here or me and Tyler here.

Marlon and Tyler are available for book signings, presentations, and workshops focusing on how to create sites for those with challenges linking their passions and encouraging others to get involved. Email for booking information.

Email: info@marlonransom.com

www.marlonransom.com

Follow Tyler's music journey on Instagram @Soulflplaying

www.healingtyler.com

THE END... FOR NOW

83259230R00049

Made in the USA
San Bernardino, CA
23 July 2018